How to Get On With Your Colleagues

T0153293

How to Get On With Your Colleagues

The School of Life

Published in 2020 by The School of Life
First published in the USA in 2021
930 High Road, London, N12 9RT

Copyright © The School of Life 2020

Designed and typeset by Marcia Mihotich
Printed in Latvia by Livonia Print

A proportion of this book has appeared online at
www.theschooloflife.com/thebookoflife

Every effort has been made to contact the copyright holders
of the material reproduced in this book. If any have been
inadvertently overlooked, the publisher will be pleased to make
restitution at the earliest opportunity.

The School of Life is a resource for helping us understand
ourselves, for improving our relationships, our careers and our
social lives – as well as for helping us find calm and get more
out of our leisure hours. We do this through creating films,
workshops, books, apps and gifts.

 www.theschooloflife.com

ISBN 978-1-912891-15-3

10 9 8 7 6 5 4

Part 1
The Need to Get
On With Others

1. Our Unhappy Past

For millennia, the idea of needing to get along with, let alone like, the people one worked alongside would have sounded absurd. Work was not an arena for friendship, self-development, meaning or pleasure. It was a curse, a biblical punishment and a necessary evil best endured with stoicism and resignation.

Workplaces were strictly hierarchical, with each person ordering about the person below them with little regard for their feelings and with a certainty that subordinates would never answer back, let alone endanger the business. The primary tool of management was the whip.

There was little choice about what job one might do. One often inherited roles; the child of a textile weaver would also become a textile weaver; the son of a lawyer would take their place in the family firm. Those in charge never asked themselves whether their workers were having an interesting time. The success of an enterprise in no way depended on whether employees found their work satisfying or to their taste.

Shouting was the best way to get anyone to do anything; it was the ideal and preferred method when trying to get labourers to dig harder, miners to push coal trolleys faster, or steelworkers to increase their rate of production at the blast furnace. A worker could feel underappreciated and bullied and nevertheless be able to perform their required tasks to perfection. Emotional distress didn't hold things up. One could operate the cotton mill at maximum speed even if one hated the manager or clean out the stables thoroughly even if one felt the foreman hadn't enquired deeply enough into the nature of one's weekend.

2. The New Cost of Unhappiness

Gradually, the world of work underwent an enormous change. It went from being primarily physical in nature to being overwhelmingly mental, dependent on our intellectual and psychological capacities as opposed to our sinews and our sweat. With this evolution came a new and, for managers, disturbing realisation: people's ability to perform their functions would now depend to a significant degree on their levels of contentment and fulfilment. How well a company might function, and therefore how profitable it could be for its investors, would critically depend on whether the junior employees felt adequately heard, a manager had a proper sense of purpose and the members of the accounts department were having a sufficiently interesting time. To their consternation, the stewards of business came to realise that they would need to start taking an interest in the mental wellbeing of those they employed.

Nowadays, without ample respect and encouragement, without a feeling of camaraderie and support, huge sums of money will be wasted on workforces and their resentment, sobbing or latent fury. Major costs, and important lost opportunities, will be entailed if a crucial member of a team can't take criticism, is sluggishly demotivated or if key figures can't manage the emotional rivalry between them. The profitability and future development of an enterprise can hang on what's happening in the head of someone sulking in the corner during a meeting or on the capacity of someone in a senior position to listen imaginatively to the mumbled concerns of a shy junior.

In the pre-psychological age, the success of enterprises depended on material factors: on access to resources, capital and technical expertise. But now, if we wanted to assess how a business might be doing in two years' time, a telling indicator might be what happened after an intern was found weeping in the bathroom or a member of the marketing team fell into a mood with their boss. If one has any concern whatsoever for the bottom line, there is no alternative but to be concerned with the psychology of the workforce.

_____ There are many options when our computers break down; few when those we work with destroy our peace of mind.

3. Gossip

That said, if there is one generalisation we can hazard about humans in the workplace, it is that they are tricky: they make too much of a fuss or not enough of one; they fail to listen or speak incessantly; they procrastinate or rush everything unduly; they grow unfeasibly furious or lack self-confidence; they backstab or dither, panic or daydream (to start the list).

We are often alone with the problems that this produces. There are many options when our computers break down; few when those we work with destroy our peace of mind. In desperation, we have one chief source of solace: we gossip. We find an ally somewhere in the team with whom to privately discharge our accumulated sorrow at the behaviour of our colleagues.

Exercise

Write down the names of three challenging people you are working (or have worked) with.

Three challenging co-workers

1

2

3

The problem with gossip in offices isn't that it happens, but that it isn't taken seriously enough. We gossip from pain and impotence; from frustration at how difficult our colleagues are combined with despair at being unable to do anything to alter dynamics other than point to the problem ironically and sigh darkly over a drink in a café around the corner from the office. Gossip is palliative; it doesn't hold out any hope for a more mature solution to our distress or a proper improvement in our workplace relationships.

But gossip is much more interesting and important than is generally understood. It reveals significant information about what is wrong inside a company and what could, with a few interventions, be put right. In its vague and elusive way, gossip circles essential topics. What we gossip about are the central themes of office psychology: we indirectly talk about communication, trust, self-worth, empathy, self-knowledge, respect, creativity and eloquence. We may not use these terms exactly; in our stories we may stick to specific people and devastating and witty takedowns of their foibles, but at heart we point to multiple failures in the arena of emotional development. It is not hard, once one starts, to perceive the psychological issues pulsing within the objects of our gossip, to identify beneath our wounded criticisms of a few maddening people a range of essential (and more universal) themes of emotional existence.

Exercise

Moving from gossip to psychological investigation.

Three challenging co-workers	What they've done	Psychological trait
1. *Aditya*	Tell marketing one thing, accounts another	*People pleasing*
2. *Mary-Jane*	Furious with Dave's report on the meeting they organised	*Defensiveness*
3. *Pablo*	Furious response to being left off an all-staff email by error	*Paranoia*

Part of what may dissuade us from delving deeper into the psychology of our colleagues is the widespread belief that offices are and should be 'professional' places. By this we mean places where people are expected to leave their personal and emotional issues behind in order to focus in on fulfilling tasks with quasi-mechanical efficiency. Although it is now thought unacceptable to try to skirt psychological issues within romantic relationships, it is still broadly expected that work should be a simpler arena where most of the complexities and sorrows of being human do not rear their heads. Once we are at our desks, we should no longer cry or panic, view our colleagues with fear or envy, focus on the person not the job, or disturb the flow of business with our accumulated oddities and compulsions.

However, we never quite manage to be self-contained and sober. Crises, passions, neuroses, jealousies, breakdowns and sulks accompany us at the office. We cannot invariably be the professionals we aspire to be; we can't neatly divide ourselves between the infinitely demanding and convoluted beings we are in our emotional lives and the ideally regulated automatons we are expected to be at work.

4. Psychotherapy at the Office

To help us cope with the complexities of the office, we have on hand a discipline not often associated with the workplace and typically relegated to private life: psychotherapy.

Psychotherapy remains one of the most valuable inventions of the last hundred years, with an exceptional power to raise our levels of emotional well-being, improve our relationships, redeem the atmosphere in our families and assist us in navigating our professional lives. If we wish to move beyond merely gossiping about our unhappy working lives and instead build companies that effectively address our emotional knots, we have few better options than to try to incorporate some of the insights of psychotherapy into our office cultures.

Psychotherapy begins with the idea that all of us are, to a greater or lesser extent, in need of its insights, for we are – often without knowing it – riddled with emotional blocks, unhelpful impulses, damaging patterns of response and self-destructive urges. We are all (without anything pejorative meant by this) *immature*.

Somewhere in childhood, our trajectory towards emotional maturity will have been impeded. Even if we had a loving childhood and were sensitively handled, we are unlikely to have reached adulthood without developing many mental reflexes that make us less than perfectly lucid, balanced and easy to interact with.

At the start of life, we are all emotionally primitive: we divide people into goodies and baddies and miss the grey; we scream

From immaturity to maturity

Immaturity	Maturity
Sulking	Explanation
Defensiveness	Learning
Refusal to teach	Becoming a good teacher
Always others' fault	Partial responsibility
People pleasing	Social courage
Paranoia/Self-hatred	Acceptance of random accident/ Self-love
Panic	Serenity/Calm
Rigid negativity	Flexible hope
Stiffness, fear of others	Charm, ease
Procrastination	Unfrightened acceptance of tasks
Cynicism	Love
Frankness	Diplomacy

or sulk rather than share our thoughts with a mixture of self-control and confidence. We become enraged when things don't go to plan and fail to realise the impact of our words on others. We have little idea of the complexity and reality of the lives of those around us. If things go wrong, it's always someone else's fault. If we are not loved properly, we don't have a robust sense of self and are likely to lack confidence and a faith that things can eventually be OK.

Maturity looks different: in this zone, people and things are rarely ever simply good or bad. We're ready to take responsibility; we're focused on communication. We resist rage or cynicism. We're diplomatic and aware of our capacity to wound others. We face the normal adversities of existence with a degree of security; we're not uprooted by every misfortune; we can cope if someone doesn't like us or disagrees with an idea that's important to us; we can put up with being sidelined on occasion and not always being the centre of attention.

All of us are stuck somewhere on the path between immaturity and its opposite, with varied progress in different subjects. We may have an emotional age of five in relation to communication, but seventy-five in relation to empathy or self-control. We may be advanced in the arena of generosity but lagging when it comes to serenity. We may be in the top set for love but the bottom set for hope.

The reasons for our blocks and warps generally come down to events in childhood. A child who was frightened of a loud, domineering parent may grow up into someone who remains internally on the defensive, lacking confidence and worrying about upsetting others. Someone with a parent who didn't listen to them properly may end up feeling that they need to be very blunt or assertive if they are to get anyone's attention. The patterns are various, but the common thread is that something that was difficult in an individual's upbringing continues to make itself felt in their grown-up working life. This is the essential story of psychotherapy,

When this goes wrong in childhood ...	... this dynamic might show up at the office
Depressed but loving parent	Reluctance to pass on difficult news: an urge to people please.
Alcoholic caregivers mired in self-pity	Tendency to focus on fanciful future hopes rather than realistic present plans: a dreamer.
A parent's career went very badly at a key stage	Hugely cautious and negative, given to pointing out why any suggestion won't work: cynic and naysayer.
A caregiver was often very busy and distracted	Always talking at meetings, starving for praise: peacock.
An irritable parent who frequently lost their temper and criticised the child unfairly	A perfectionist who won't admit to mistakes: manically defensive.
Daunting parents who never allowed the child to feel at home in their own skin	A lack of charm; a stiffness of manner; unnatural and inauthentic.

which seeks to help people by guiding them to understand the intimate history behind the troubles of their adult existence.

Maddeningly for our desire to be simple and 'professional', ordinary troubles in our early years can lead to tricky behaviour at work.

The list of problems and their origins is humbling in its potential length. Yet the strength of the connections between present behaviour and past experience has a redemptive and humane side. For the more we can understand what drives our actions and feelings – and those of others – the more we can explain, forgive and be forgiven. We can move from seeing tricky behaviour as merely weird or cruel to conceiving of it in richer and kinder terms.

In an emotionally literate office, it will be broadly accepted that everyone in a team will bring certain immaturities into their working lives. No one was perfectly parented and so everyone bears (more or less openly) a range of inner wounds that will affect their attitudes and behaviours. Knowing this invites one to engage a vital degree of psychological wisdom where there might otherwise only have been loneliness, irritation or impatience.

Until more or less now, it never seemed obvious that thinking about people's early histories could have much to do with running a business or working in an office. It still feels odd. But the rationale is direct: to operate successfully within a complex modern organisation we need to get on with one another, but we won't be able to do so properly until we can find a language to identify and define our psychological immaturities (without embarrassment or shame) and are then able to address them collectively in a supportive and open-minded atmosphere. This is what it will mean to build emotionally intelligent offices.

5. Beyond Gossip

None of us is mature. What follows is a series of sketches of the ways in which we all behave less than optimally. Some of them will be traits we find difficult in others; others we will see in ourselves. We should, when identified, wince warm-heartedly or laugh from the kindest sort of recognition, rather than assume we are being got at; we are invariably implicated in some area or another, to a greater or lesser extent, so there is no need to feel unfairly singled out. It is open to all of us to put ourselves on a path to improvement once we can face up to our flaws with courage.

While all of us are infinitely various, defining immaturities by type should help us to spot clusters of symptoms and grant us an insight into others beyond a feeling that they are simply 'annoying' or 'mean'. It is too easy to say that someone is a brute or a fool, an idiot or a jerk, as opposed to attempting imaginatively to recreate what might be happening in their minds to make them as they are. We should exchange gossip for a move towards collegial relationships founded on honest dialogue, psychological maturity and self-knowledge.

_____ We should exchange gossip for a move towards collegial relationships founded on honest dialogue, psychological maturity and self-knowledge.

Part 2
The Challenges

1

Defensiveness

i. A character study

They are by nature extremely efficient. They make an especially good impression in the early days. They might be the first one into the office and the last to leave. They were expected to deliver a report at the end of the week and by Tuesday midday it's already been done. Their desk is immaculate.

But then, slowly, a problem rears its head. Their report was impressive in areas and beautifully presented throughout. However, there were a few things missing, as one would expect, given that this is only their second week with the company. It would have been nice to integrate some of the sales data and perhaps to use a few pie charts to make the conclusions stand out.

So, along with the praise, you mention how a second draft might look. But no sooner have you begun than you are surprised to receive an immediate, curt and distinctly wounded: 'Of course'. You want to explain further, but when you start again, you are cut off with a clipped: 'Yes, no problem at all'. Then comes an abrupt and urgent, 'I understand completely'. Having to hear your account of what they didn't grasp and might want to amend is almost unbearable; it seems that if they could, they would block their ears and start humming. You have, inadvertently, invited a defensive non-listener onto the team.

The attendant challenges start to mount. Whenever you suggest the potential for improvement, they either deny that there's anything wrong or implausibly assert that they also just realised there was a problem and were about to fix it. You sense a sulk brewing every time you need to speak. If you persist in trying to highlight a worrying area, they develop sharp-edged reasons why the problem exists only in your imagination. The price of feedback rises exponentially. In certain moods, they go on the offensive: they query why you are raising this now (when they have worked so hard); they insinuate that you are getting at them unfairly (they are doing everything they can) and point out that you are the only one to have a problem with them (everyone in marketing is happy with their work).

The defensive non-listener is a perfectionist; that is, someone with an unusually intense and intractable commitment to getting everything right. While this might seem to have its advantages (it could be an asset to have someone who cares so much), perfectionism becomes problematic when it brings with it an inability to listen to what may have gone wrong at the first attempt; when it becomes the cause for an upset over anything less than immediately laudable. The defensive perfectionist, despite their dread of failure, paradoxically cannot bring themselves to take ideas on board and thereby bring their output closer to the perfection they so desire. They will do anything other than take the one step that would be so beneficial to them and those they live and work with: *admit to a problem and see what could be done to put it right.*

ii. Origins

The reluctance to acknowledge fault is so intense for the non-listener because, in their minds, not-already-knowing and making the slightest error have unconsciously become associated with catastrophe. There is perpetually a vast gulf open between what one tells them and what they can hear.

What is said to them	What they hear
It would be great to increase the margin size.	You don't deserve to exist.
Have you thought of adding some extra presentation documents?	Why can you never do anything right?
Maybe we should try to get the data in by the middle of the month in future.	You're a lazy, disorganised wretch.

The psychology of the defensive non-listener was generally established a long time ago. One of the stranger features of adulthood is that we interpret and respond to people in ways that are determined not by the here and now but by certain experiences we went through as children. Our minds seem not always to know what the time is or who we are dealing with. Ostensibly, we understand that we are in the office in the present but, in our unconscious, we may still be back in the nursery in the old house three decades before.

Where we are

Where the unconscious thinks we are

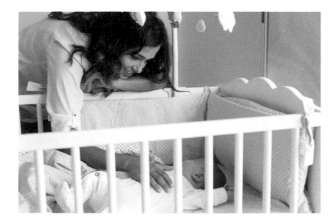

A confusion about who we are talking to

Boss now

Father then

In the case of the defensive, although they might grasp objectively that they are having a conversation with their boss, their unconscious may lead them to behave as if their interlocutor might be their father, who is about to punish them just as he did when they were small.

Psychotherapy has an array of tests that show up the presence of the unknown past and, with it, our proclivity to impose (or, as the technical term puts it, to 'transfer') old assumptions and patterns of thinking onto contemporary reality. The best known of such tests, devised in the 1930s by the Swiss psychologist Hermann Rorschach, presents us with groups of ambiguous images generated by spilt ink, upon which we're asked to reflect without inhibition, expressing freely what we feel of their atmosphere and identity.

Rorschach's images have no predetermined meaning. They aren't about anything in particular; they are suggestive in a vast array of directions, so the atmospheres we see in them depend upon what our pasts most readily predispose us to feel. To an individual who inherited from their parents a kindly and forgiving conscience, a given image might be viewed as a sweet mask, with eyes, floppy ears, a covering for the mouth and wide flaps extending from the cheeks. Another, hounded across childhood by a domineering father, could view it as a powerful figure seen from below, with splayed feet, thick legs, heavy shoulders and a head bent forward as if poised for attack. Bosses themselves too often function a little like a Rorschach blotch, triggering unconscious expectations of how people in authority might treat us.

Hermann Rorschach,
Inkblot test, 1932

Exercise

This exercise indicates how we superimpose the past on the present. Your boss unexpectedly asks you to step into their office. What's your first instinctive reaction? What do you imagine is going to happen?

(a) They want to ask my advice about something I know quite a lot about.

(b) There is probably a new project coming up that they want to discuss.

(c) They might be going to promote me.

(d) They are angry with me about something. They see me as a liability and a shameful person; there's a chance they will fire me.

Finally: How did you get on with authority figures in childhood?

The specific details of a childhood that fostered defensive non-listening will always have a local colour and accent to them, but they can be guaranteed to have one thing in common: at some point in the past of the non-listener, getting things wrong (failing in the broad sense) will have been experienced as appallingly and (seemingly) life-threateningly dangerous. Maybe there was a parent who grew enraged at the slightest error, who shouted violently when things were not quite right and gave the child a sense that they might want to do away with them for being less than perfect. Or maybe there was a parent who was kind yet weak and seemed in danger of collapse if we disappointed them or couldn't support them through extraordinary accomplishments. Or else there was a parent who was self-sacrificial and had a way of ushering in guilt for any errors one made, and conveyed that one would be a terrible, ungrateful person if one disappointed them in any way.

As a result, whenever there is criticism, there is also a memory of fierce attack and huge risks, which starts to explain the strength of the denial with which feedback is greeted. In the early years, there was no reliable boundary between the local idea of having failed at a task and the more general idea of being a worthless being, which is why the stakes around a minor comment continue to feel so high.

Without meaning to be, the defensive non-listener is a liar. Yet the more we understand about the origin of the need to lie, the more benevolently we can feel towards those who end up doing so in relation to feedback. Plato once outlined an idea of what he called the 'just lie'. If a crazed person comes to us asking for an axe, we can feel entitled to claim that we don't have one even if we do; we understand that, were we to tell the truth, they would use the tool to do something horrendous to us. In other words, we can reasonably tell a lie when our life seems in danger.

Our life is not generally at risk at the office: a boss will not want to swing at us with an axe when they ask a searching question about a project. But, psychologically, this is precisely how the defensive person may experience the enquiry; this makes it understandable that they might say that there isn't a problem and that the report is completely fine as it is. The defensive person cannot help but fear that their mistakes will be used as a weapon against them. They might long to admit to all that is imperfect about their work, but they never feel sufficiently safe to undertake the process. They are so burdened with shame and guilt already that a colleague's comment, however delicate, feels impossible to listen to. There is too much pre-existing fragility in their psyches for them to own up to yet another difficult insight into what might be wrong with them.

When you were a child, what was the dominant message you received in response to your errors?

1. *Don't worry, it's fine, everyone makes mistakes. (Forgiveness)*
2. *How could you be so stupid, idiot. (Aggression)*
3. *I've done so much for you; is this fair? (Guilt)*

iii. Ways forward

To help the defensive non-listener to lessen their fears, a priority is to try to alter their underlying sense of what it means to make a mistake. We need to humanise error and show that it belongs in the lives of all good and admirable people. Ideally, the most senior members of a company would be encouraged to detail their failings in a public forum and to explore their omissions and blunders without judgement, in an atmosphere of benevolent good humour and cheerful pessimism. Within a working team, messing up would be viewed not as a freakish anomaly that deserves to be punished with cruelty and sarcasm, but as something that happens naturally whenever intelligent people gather to take on a complex task.

Part of the challenge is to get the non-listener to admit that they might be defensive in the first place. The best recourse is to frame the quirk in general and non-pejorative terms rather than in individual and shameful ones. It should be stated as an unsurprising and unembarrassing fact of human nature that everyone has defensive non-listening tendencies and that the prestigious and adult move is to admit to the phenomenon with speed and grace. It is as normal to try to shut one's ears to challenging information as it is to slip into sad or irritable moods. To counter the persecutory psyche of the defensive person, the management might simply hang a sign above the door that reads: *We are all (at points) a bit defensive here.*

Exercise

We all have things that we suspect are true about us that we can't bear to confront, let alone hear about from others (that we are a little paranoid, judgemental with others or self-pitying...). With great kindness to ourselves, on a sheet of paper, list a few of these negative traits. Complete the sentence: A few awful things about me that I generally don't confront are...

....

....

....

We're trying to practise the little-known art of acknowledging our less admirable, more immature shadow sides. Doing this in the company of other people should let us see that we are not alone in our frailties and lend us courage to listen a little more and block our ears a little less.

The defensive person has been cursed with a conviction that failures, mistakes and errors cannot be forgiven; in line with their formative experiences, they imagine that others will always be shocked by and severe about their less-than-perfect actions. We need to show them otherwise: to help them to see that what happened to them in childhood was not representative of what normally occurs between most adults in a working context and that the catastrophe they fear has already happened to them and therefore need not be warded off in situations that don't warrant it.

Along the way, we need to encourage the defensive non-listener to feel compassion for themselves for what happened long ago. We need to be careful that they do not end up feeling even more ashamed of themselves the more they learn about the origins of their behaviour. Their brittleness is not a sign of arrogance, simply a response to traumatic incidents. They should, in safe circumstances, revisit these in their minds, experiencing a newfound kindness for the vulnerable small person they once were – a child who needed to be perfect because circumstances were too harsh to allow them to be merely good enough.

At the same time, we need to take the defensive non-listener into the mindset of people who give them feedback and broaden their impression of why others call them in for chats. The inner conviction of the defensive is that their critics are motivated by a desire to wound and humiliate, and that any criticism means they are no good. We can show them that, within a working context, there is generally only one reason why criticism occurs: in order for a business to function more effectively. Commercial organisations have no systematic desire or incentive to shame their employees; they have a much more humane and more urgent task at hand – that of fulfilling their customers and improving their profits.

We need to help the defensive to appreciate the extent to which they have allowed themselves to hear only the aggressive interpretation of any comments on their work and remind them of the true and innocent meaning of most of what will be said to them.

A: What they tell me	B: What it sounds like	C: What it really means
Do add the final figures to the presentation.	You are an idiot.	Do add the final figures to the presentation.
It would be good always to try to start the meeting at 5 p.m.	You disappoint and disgust me.	It would be good always to try to start the meeting at 5 p.m.

Being defensive does not spring from arrogance or pride. It is the adult relic of a childhood fear of what could happen if a mistake were to be admitted, projected into situations where such risks no longer apply. A few others may once long ago have questioned our right to exist every time we erred; we should mourn the difficult long-gone years but then dare to believe that we have entered a more benevolent, goal-oriented and forgiving present.

_____ Being defensive does not spring from arrogance or pride. It is the adult relic of a childhood fear of what could happen if a mistake were to be admitted, projected into situations where such risks no longer apply.

Perhaps oddly, emotional growth requires a good deal of practice. We all need to practise hearing true but uncomfortable things about ourselves. Hand a colleague the list of your flaws you outlined in the previous exercise. Ask them to read these back to you. Get used to hearing feedback without flinching or suspecting that the speaker is doing anything other than trying to get something done.

2
Poor Teaching

i. A character study

This member of the team, who is probably also a manager, is constantly cross with colleagues. Why are they surrounded by morons? Why do other employees not get it more quickly? Why can't they work as precisely and swiftly as they themselves can? Last week, three people completely failed to grasp how to draw up the portfolios for the Dutch clients, even though it should have been clear from the three-line instruction they were sent at the start of the month. Then there's the new recruit in the sales department, who keeps misreading what's needed and sends gormless off-target emails that show a thorough misunderstanding of how the business functions. And that's not to mention the numbskulls in the regional office or the idiots in recruitment.

The Roman Emperor Nero, when he was culling his insubordinate staff, complained at how long it was taking to punish them in his usual style. 'I wish you Romans had only one neck,' screamed the aggrieved Nero. Execution would be going a bit far, of course, but, on some days in the office, the non-teacher can concur with the feeling.

To get around their disappointment with other people, the non-teacher spends a lot of time on secret manoeuvres: they give up on those they are meant to be collaborating with, fail to talk to them about their disappointments, and instead work around them with the help of a few select not-always-officially-sanctioned colleagues. The secretly manoeuvring non-teacher may seem supportive in meetings and may appear to have taken a suggestion on board quite positively. But behind the scenes, they are determined to find another route. They set up secret side groups. It's meant to be a collaboration between twenty equals, but they go out and hire two external consultants without telling anyone. It sounds Machiavellian, but it's more sorrowful than that; it's the outcome of a terrible lack of faith in the power of communication.

In their personal life, the non-teacher may well have a lover as well as a spouse: they're disappointed with the partner they married, but they haven't come around to expressing what they really feel. It's not their style; it seemed better to steer around the conflict and start up a new relationship on the side. They're doing in business a version of what they're doing in their marriage. They're devoting themselves to 'lovers' because they can't tolerate the idea of instructing the group to which they pledged themselves originally.

ii. Origins

Beneath these behaviours lies one central issue: a disdain for teachers. In theory, we pay lip service to the value of the teaching profession, but in practice, many of us suspect that teaching is a dull and lowly occupation that we were glad to have moved away from once we graduated. The pace, remuneration and stylish atmosphere of many modern businesses is a welcome far cry from the fustiness of the classroom; we may secretly pity the poor types in sensible jackets who are currently drilling new generations in the intricacies of long division and French irregular verbs.

And yet, whatever one's background fears, teaching is one of the most central, unavoidable and noble aspects of existence. Even if we haven't signed up to instruct adolescents in algebra or to coax five-year-olds to read, we are called upon to 'teach' almost every hour of every day. We have to teach others how we're feeling, what we want, what is paining us, and, in the context of work, what we think needs doing and how. The specialist subject we undertake to teach throughout our lives is that bizarre-sounding yet enormous topic: *Who I Am, How I Feel and What I Care About.*

Unfortunately, most of us are terrible teachers. We don't explain calmly or thoroughly; we don't maintain good humour or spare our 'bad' pupils punishment. We blame people for not already knowing what we have never deigned to tell them. We end up seething with resentment at their ongoing ignorance (as to the way to format an introductory letter, budget or chat to a client) but never take the steps required to correct it. We are furious with colleagues for not knowing things that we assume they should know without ever having been taught. We fail to get others to see what matters so much to us: why we are enraged when people speak out of turn at a meeting; why endless committees are not required to get a project done; why we hate their tone in presentations.

What we think of as a specific professional skill that belongs in school is actually a key form of communication, and a basic human requirement for the healthy operation of any community, relationship or office.

Despairing of teaching, saying nothing and then going behind people's backs doesn't sound kind when stated baldly. But for many it is not an unreasonable strategy given our childhood circumstances. At an early stage, the non-teacher probably came up against the futility – and indeed impossibility – of directly asserting their needs and interests. There was no way to complain. Those tasked with caring for them were too preoccupied, troubled or volatile to take their requirements on board. Straightforward conversation would have been either useless or plain dangerous. The only option was therefore to remain quiet and then try to outwit key figures behind their backs.

Exercise

We are often out of touch with just how distinctive our childhoods were and how little we might have been allowed to express our genuine needs and fears.

Without thinking too much (allowing the unconscious to have its say), complete the following sentences:

- *If I told my mother/father what I really thought, they would...*
- *What I learnt about communication in my childhood is...*
- *Complaining is...*
- *If you tell people what you really feel...*

We understand well enough how, in military campaigns, faced with an overpowering adversary, the weaker side will avoid a pitched battle at all costs. The same holds true for the non-teacher, for whom taking an indirect route – not asking for help, not openly disagreeing, dismissing all hope of persuading others – was often the only option.

iii. Ways forward

What we call 'teaching' is the complex, noble art of getting an idea, insight, emotion or skill from one human brain into another. Whatever the subject matter, the elements of this skill tend to be the same.

Most of us have probably started off by being quite bad teachers. This is nothing to be ashamed of: like most things, teaching can, and must, be learnt. What, then, are some of the prerequisites of the good teacher?

The first priority is to stay calm in the face of their ignorance: the person being taught should not feel scared, angry or hurt. No one learns well when they are insulted, threatened or humiliated. Few of us can take ideas properly on board when the insinuation is that we are a fool. In order to be receptive to teaching we need to be comforted that the teacher has patience for us, reassured of our value and given licence to fail.

In order for teachers to achieve calm, they must recognise the legitimacy of ignorance. Certain ideas can seem so important, we can't imagine that others don't already know them. We suspect that they may be deliberately upsetting us by pretending not to know. This attitude makes it unlikely that what needs to be taught will make its way successfully into the other person's head. Good teaching relies on the idea that ignorance is not a defect of the individual being instructed: it's the consequence of never having been properly taught. So the fault really belongs with the person who hasn't done enough to get the required ideas into others' heads: in other words, with the teacher. Often, that's us.

Good teachers are able to tolerate the frustration generated by the ignorance of others without bursting into fury. The more we need other people to know something, the less we may be able to secure the serene frame of mind that is indispensable if we are to have a chance of conveying it to them effectively. The possibility that they won't quickly understand something that matters to us can drive us into agitation – the worst state in which to conduct any lesson. By the time we've started to insult our so-called pupil, to call them a blockhead or a fool, the lesson is over.

Paradoxically, the best sort of teachers can tolerate the possibility that what they have to teach will not be understood. This slightly detached, slightly pessimistic approach stands the best chance of generating the relaxed frame of mind essential to successful pedagogy.

Another skill of good teachers is that they can admit that they don't know lots of things. It can be crushing to be in the learning position. Someone else has information you don't. This can be belittling; the person learning may shut their ears and hate the alleged superiority of the one in the teaching role. So the good teacher knows to admit that they are, in many areas of life, themselves pretty ignorant. This might seem to undermine their authority. Far from it: it creates an atmosphere of goodwill and modesty that puts the learner at ease. They might not know this particular thing that is being taught but they are, overall, not inferior to the 'teacher'. They can dare to face up to their ignorance in a given area and submit to the discipline of having it corrected.

Λ good teacher will not wait until the problem arises to teach a lesson, but selects a time when it is likely to be well received. Crises aren't the best times for a lesson. We might have to wait a long time – three days after a heated discussion, for example – in order to pick just the opportune occasion to deal with its underlying dynamics. When our colleague is having their lunch break and humming a song might be the wisest moment cheerfully and innocently to refer back to something that agitated us a little while back, but over which we were sagely silent at the time.

As we're beginning to see, the more desperate we feel, the less likely we are to get through to others effectively. It is unfortunate that we usually end up addressing the most complex and crucial teaching tasks just when we feel most irritated and under pressure. We suffer from a panicked feeling that if we don't jump on this right now, an issue will go on unchecked forever. We should be more confident that not jumping on an issue is what will allow us to fix it properly a little way down the line.

Good teachers are also good 'students'. They know that everyone has a lot to learn and that more or less everyone has something important to impart. Valuable knowledge can reside in unexpected locations within hierarchical organisations. The intern who joined only last week may have some crucial insights it would be wise for the CEO to listen to. Only a perfect being would be committed to staying just as they are.

Finally, good teachers who had difficult pasts are committed to overcoming their acquired pessimism and desire to find an expedient way around those who cause them problems. They recognise that their team member is not their difficult parent, and might, if the lessons are delivered to them correctly, be transformed in their abilities. They have faith in others' potential to learn.

We are the unconscious inheritors of a Romantic tradition that encourages a suspicion of teaching outside of narrowly technical fields. It can sound weird or impossible to try to 'teach' someone to adopt a more sober tone in their documents, to alter their response to new ideas or to approach difficulty with greater resilience. We fail to teach because we're not alive to the variety, possibility and importance of the teaching task.

A close-up look at a rough
pegmatite stone

Exercise

The non-teacher often has a clear picture in their minds of what they want, but lacks a corresponding awareness of how hard it is for others to know the contents of their minds, and therefore how hard they will need to work to teach them. They automatically assume that others know.

To shake ourselves from this assumption, we might look closely at this image of a rock.

We should then find a colleague who hasn't seen it and try to describe it to them in as much detail as we can, detailing shape, texture, formation and so on. After a few moments, we should then show them the image and ask them to rate (on a scale of 1–10) how well we conveyed what the rock looks like. This can be a useful lesson in the challenges of explaining to others what is in our minds even when (or precisely because) the information is clear to us.

Exercise

We become better at tricky things with practice. The secretly manoeuvring non-teacher hasn't had enough practice being direct and politely assertive; this option hasn't been allowed in their difficult past. This exercise is designed to give the behind-the-scenes operator in all of us a chance to rehearse a different approach.

Imagine that you are an actor in a play. You've been cast as an assertive, direct person; you're not aggressive, you don't insult or make trouble, you just quietly lay out what's on your mind. You know how to teach.

Unfortunately, there's a hitch. The scriptwriter hasn't finalised your lines and in rehearsal you will have to ad lib. How do you play the character when:

- *Someone barges in front of you in a queue?*
- *Your boss has asked you to do something you don't totally understand? Ask for clarification.*
- *Your partner suggests an unwelcome change to domestic arrangements (inviting unwelcome people to dinner)?*
- *A capable new person is appointed to a role that overlaps with your own and you are discussing the change with your boss?*

3

People Pleasing

i. A character study

The people-pleaser at first appears to be the ideal colleague and human. They are always smiling, they are well turned out, they are eager to help, they immediately back up your hunches, and they concur with almost everything you say. 'I agree' is one of their favourite phrases. You tend to leave interactions with them cheered by how kind and thoughtful they are and buoyed up by how sensible and clever they've made you feel.

But then you start to note some more troubling signals. Last week, they agreed with you on a contentious issue in the office, but you discover that they've spoken to some other people since then and now apparently agree with their views instead. When you catch up with them at lunchtime and ask them in a puzzled tone where they stand, they blush, look pained and tell you that they do still agree with you. You're left with a disturbing impression that they would simply side with whoever they happened to be standing next to at the cafeteria.

Then there's their attitude to difficult news. They're handling a big technology project that everyone is waiting for. You ask them several times if all is progressing well and are told the news you'd longed to hear: the project will be ready dead on time. For a while, you let down your guard and anticipate success, which renders you all the more surprised and defenceless when, half a day before the supposed launch – when it's too late to take any averting action – the people-pleaser announces that there's been a big delay.

After a few questions, it emerges that they'd known about this for a month already; they just hadn't wanted to disturb anyone with the challenging information.

They are mortified by our distress. More than anyone, they know the suffering that comes from not being able to please other people. At the same time, they are on the way to annoying and troubling a sizeable number of their colleagues.

ii. Origins

On the face of it, being someone who pleases people sounds like a good idea. But it is a pattern of behaviour riddled with pitfalls, as much for the perpetrator as for their colleagues. The people-pleaser is someone (who might at times be oneself) who feels they have no option but to mould themselves to the expectations of others, even if doing so can lead a person to conceal their real emotions – a route that can ultimately lead to mutinous resentment. They confuse everyone around them by failing to express, in due time and with the requisite courage, their authentic needs and ambitions.

At times it can feel as if the people-pleaser's attitude of smiling assent is nothing short of fake. Yet the people-pleaser is faking for poignant reasons: not in order to gain advantage, but because they are terrified of the displeasure of others.

To understand and sympathise with the people-pleaser, we need to look at their past: this almost invariably involves an early experience of being around someone – usually a parent – who seemed unable to accept them as they were.

Perhaps their father flew into volcanic rage at any sign of disobedience. Perhaps their mother sulked for days if they refused to wear a chosen dress. To eat, think or behave in a different way, even to own up to tiredness or anxiety, was to risk annihilation or the withdrawal of the love on which they depended. To survive, they needed to be acutely responsive to what others expected them to do and say.

A people-pleaser may not always fake out of fear; it was also often out of love for someone they were profoundly attached to but who was vulnerable in some way. They faked responses out of a longing not to set off another row, a desire to keep a depressive parent in a good mood, or to avoid further burdening what seemed like an already difficult or sad life. On some level, they needed to protect someone they cared about from the complications of reality.

It is no wonder that, in adulthood, the people-pleaser might find it easier to second-guess what someone else might want than to fathom their own desires.

iii. Ways forward

Now grown up, and in the workplace, the people-pleaser is operating on an out-of-date belief system. As colleagues we might gently suggest to them the following ideas:

The first is that their colleagues, partners and friends are almost certainly very different from the people around whom their anxieties evolved in childhood. Most adult humans can cope quite well with a bit of contradiction, a dose of unwelcome information or an occasional rejection, when delivered with requisite politeness. The truth will not make us explode or dissolve. The people from whom they learned their particular way of relating to the world may not be representative of all humanity.

The second is that they may have absorbed a skewed notion of what might actually be helpful to other people, derived from the distinctive needs of the particular individuals they had to cope with. Maybe their difficult parents responded well to ingratiating compliments, however insincere; maybe they were placated by good news, even if the real information was buried. These moves worked then but they are not, to most people, particularly attractive; nor are they helpful in the workplace.

They may also be unaware of the inadvertently harmful side effects of their 'kind' behaviour. They may genuinely have good intentions, but when we are not open with our thoughts and feelings, we endanger everyone. At work, we aren't doing anyone a service by withholding our doubts and agreeing to something we can't deliver, just as in love there is no kindness in staying in a relationship simply because it seems the other might not survive without us: they will. Saying what you think someone wants to hear can be wasting their time, energy and goodwill.

Finally, we can learn to be more honest by acquiring what can be counted as the art of imparting difficult messages. As children, we couldn't give nuance to the points we needed to make. We didn't know how to craft our raw pain and needs into convincing explanations. Now, it is open to us to be firm in our own views but amiable as well. We can say 'no' reasonably and without hostility; we can say someone is wrong without implying that they are an idiot. In other words, we can be pleasant without being people-pleasers.

Once we understand the people-pleaser better and can sympathetically grasp why they behave as they do, those around them can also work to assuage their counterproductive fears. The key is to lessen their sense of the price of disagreement and of not doing what others want. We can explain to people-pleasers that we don't mind if they have a divergent point of view; that we can distinguish the messenger from the message; that we'd rather know now than next month if there is a delay, and that it's reasonable for someone to say they are overstretched when they are. We're seeking to normalise, in their mind, the idea of being the cause of problems and difficulties for others. Making a few people a bit disgruntled for a time is an ordinary aspect of being an interesting and productive person, and might, in the long run, be the only basis for genuinely contributing to the delight and assistance of others.

Exercise

Practise tempering your own people pleasing tendencies. Have a go at saying some difficult yet sensitive things to others:

- *Your boss asks you to take on a new project. Your hands are already full. Let them know, asking them what their top priorities are.*

- *Someone is throwing themselves a big birthday party far away. You're exhausted and can't face going. Role play the phone call.*

- *After a few dates, you realise the other person wants to see you again, but you'd rather not. Let them down firmly but gently.*

- *Your colleague eats snacks all through the day. In an open-plan office, the rustling and chomping makes it impossible to concentrate. How do you let them know?*

4
Paranoia

i. A character study

It is surely an advantage to be a little suspicious of people one doesn't know too well, and alert to the possibility that one might in certain office contexts end up being undermined or kept away from opportunities. But something more extreme and poignant can also be at play. There is the colleague who is perpetually certain that they are being mocked, taken for granted, ridiculed, surrounded by plotters, sidelined and sabotaged, and insinuates as much to their ever more confused and exhausted fellow employees.

A group email inviting this person to a meeting to discuss future options has failed to reach them. There can be only one explanation: they are deliberately being excluded by jealous team members. Someone they are relying on for an answer has not got back to them: it must be because they have decided to make their life miserable and is attempting to punish them. This person oversees a part of a website that is meant to be updated every Friday by three people they manage. It's Sunday morning and the new items haven't appeared; it must be some kind of insurrection that needs to be dealt with by a round of aggressive and furious emails.

They know that management books and articles talk about the need for 'trust', but the concept has always seemed alien. There is generally only one explanation for all the irritations, delays, ambiguities, failures and errors of office life: that their many co-workers are essentially malevolent. Why would one trust? Why wait to discover the facts and hold out for possibly innocent reasons? There are very few benign mistakes; there are plots, there is rage and there is villainy. No wonder many of the emails they send out are abrupt and regrettably aggressive.

ii. Origins

It looks as if the paranoid person hates everyone, but this is too direct and literal a judgement. The real target of their suspicion lies closer to home: it is themselves they hate. It isn't that they are living in an exceptionally unreliable or slippery office world; it is that they despise themselves with rare and forensic intensity.

The logic, at its simplest, goes like this: if we feel, deep down, like a piece of rubbish whose very existence is unwanted, it then seems plausible that enemies will plot to destroy us, that fellow team members will scrutinise and undermine us, that our manager will sideline us and that we should be imminently disgraced and mocked by embittered clients.

Such eventualities are in the realm of the possible for anyone, but for those who hate themselves, they shift to being near certainties. As the internal logic has it, very bad things must necessarily happen to very bad people. Those who don't like themselves will expect awful events to befall them, and will worry intensely whenever, for some peculiar reason, things aren't catastrophic – yet. It is surely only a matter of time until this mistake is corrected (few things are as panic-inducing to a self-hater as apparently good news).

Paranoia is a symptom of disgust at one's own being. The difficulty is that most of us who hate ourselves are not aware of it. The feeling that we are a horrific person is merely a given, no longer worth examining. It is the default setting of the paranoid's personality rather than a visible distortion that we might observe as it goes about ruining our life. It sounds absurd to the self-hating person to claim that they might be angry with their colleague because they hate themselves. They are simply certain that there was sarcasm in the tone of their colleague's last email. Likewise, the self-hating boss doesn't think that they are constantly worried about the opinion of their staff because they are so far from picturing themselves as a fitting target for widespread respect; they're merely upset that the reception to their company-wide speech was underwhelming.

iii. Ways forward

The first step towards breaking the cycle of paranoia is for the self-hater to notice when they are behaving as if they are convinced that they deserve misery, and to see that this self-assessment colours most of their assessments of their fellow humans. If this is us, we should start to observe (without blaming ourselves) how often we are driven to interpret ambiguity as fuelled by the darkest possible motives.

Exercise

A colleague has failed to send out an email they promised to work on last week. Which explanation most readily comes to mind?

1. *It was a mistake.*
2. *It seems odd but it's worth waiting to find out what happened.*
3. *This is outrageous mockery on the part of someone having a laugh at our expense.*

If 3, we might wonder: how much do we like ourselves?

How might a self-loving person behave and look at matters in the same shoes? If to the paranoid self-hater the logic of their interpretation seems inalienable, a better tack might be to wonder how a person who liked themselves might think in the same position. Freed from shame and the reflex instinct to make themselves feel bad, how would they view the situation?

Work, with its competing demands and personality conflicts, is rich with ambiguities, gaps in knowledge, delays and silences that are immediately filled in a negative direction by the self-hater. But what if they tried to size up a given situation more neutrally, without the pitilessness of one convinced they were owed a shameful response? The result might be less aggressive behaviour, which for once might not be met with the reaction the self-hater's worst fears have predicted.

A dialogue with another person might be helpful. An outside eye, of a good friend or, ideally, a good therapist, can break us out of the closed system of our own interpretations and help us to notice just how peculiar and masochistic our analyses are.

To correct self-hatred and shame is a life's task. We are back to an all-too-familiar theme: that most psychological problems arise because people have not been empathetically cherished and reliably loved when it really mattered, and that if one could be granted one wish to improve the internal well-being of humanity, then it would be, with a wave of a magic wand, to do away with shame. The collective gasp of relief would be heard on distant galaxies – and in offices worldwide.

5
Panickiness

i. A character study

Every new office day brings with it revelations of things that are not quite as they should be: the contract with the Italian supplier has been delayed. There's a problem with the accounts. The paper stock still hasn't arrived. One will need to change venue for the seminar...

In relation to such setbacks, there are always options for how to respond. But to one particular kind of colleague, there is only ever one plausible way: panic.

The moment the bad news arrives signals the end of all peace, certainty, composure and confidence. There is instead a rapid heartbeat, a flushed face, a shortness of breath and an inclination to reply to anyone who tells them not to worry by saying that they simply don't understand what is at stake.

No one doubts that there are setbacks. The problem is that for one kind of person, there are only ever disasters, combined with imminent calamity.

ii. Origins

It's the middle of the night, let's imagine, and we've been on the earth for about three months. A lot is still unclear. We are helpless, barely able to move our own head, and at the mercy of others. The sources of our suffering and joy lie far outside our understanding. Powerful needs course through us at regular intervals and we have no way of making sense of them to ourselves, let alone of communicating them reliably to others.

A minute ago, we were asleep in a dark enveloping warmth. Now we're awake, bereft, isolated and uncomfortable. There seems to be a pain somewhere in our stomach, but the agony is more general; we are lonely and profoundly sad. The room is dark and there's a mysterious set of shadows on the wall that appear and vanish at random.

In a rising panic, we start to scream out in the darkness. Nothing happens. We pause to recover our breath and then scream even louder. Our lungs strain with the effort. Still nothing and the darkness and loneliness grow ever more threatening. Now true desperation sets in; this feels like the end of everything good and true, and we scream as if to ward off death.

At last, just when it seems we could not go on any further, the door opens. A warm orange light is turned on. It is a familiar face. They smile at us, say the name they often use around us, pick us up and put us against their shoulder. We can hear a familiar heart beating next to ours and a warm hand caressing the top of our head. They gently move us to and fro, and sing a tender, sweet song. Our sobs start to abate, we pull a weak smile; it feels as if the vicious demons and merciless goblins have been sent packing, and that life could be bearable after all.

Soothing is one of the kindest gestures that humans ever perform for one another. It lies at the heart of love, of how one human can relate to another, and is what can make the difference between a desire to die and the capacity to endure.

We can soothe ourselves. But it tends to be hard to do so unless we have first – usually in childhood – experienced being soothed by someone else. A capacity for self-soothing is the legacy of a history of nurture. If we have been scooped up and calmed enough times early on, and sufficiently reassured in the midst of panic that it is all OK, we will make it, then one part of our minds learns the art and in time can practise it on the other, and eventually, on people outside us too.

If we know what it is to be soothed, at moments of crisis, we can access an internal voice that calms the waves of fear and the blows of panic. We can tell ourselves: *you can sort this out; you can have a conversation with them; there's still time to fix it*. We find within ourselves an unflustered, resolute response to both the most awful events and to routine panics. We have faith that we can endure, that something will show up and that we don't deserve the worst.

iii. Ways forward

Reflecting on the art of soothing may bring into focus just how much we are missing. We are not mysteriously or uniquely deficient; we were brought up by adults who were themselves not soothed.

For the non-soothed, life often feels much harder than it should be; every setback feels frightening, disapproval feels fatal, ambiguity unbearable, sleep feels unearned and holidays seem superfluous – too many of our days and nights are rocked by what feel like near-death experiences. Whether in our own self, or observing others, we need to treat this missing part of the psyche with deep and attentive sympathy: at a vital and powerless time, an experience that enables a person to respond with confidence and some control to the inevitable mishaps that unfold in complex lives was missed.

Yet there are, one must believe, substitutes and opportunities for catching up. We all have recourse to music, diaries, beds, baths and, most importantly, other people. However, seeking out the sort of people who can soothe us may be the hardest step. If we were not brought up to expect comfort, we may mistake a capacity to soothe for weakness or naivety. We may take the soother for a fool. We may need soothing so much, we find ourselves unable to ask for it nicely, shouting counterproductively instead, or else we withdraw into defensive independence, because help feels as if it hasn't come soon enough. Those in the greatest need of soothing often have no sensible way of articulating their need, and a dogged suspicion of kindness when it is offered.

For the panicker in the workplace, the greatest comfort may be reality. Taking a deep breath, we should notice how much scarier things are in our own minds than they actually turn out to be, and how many things can go wrong every day without ushering in the calamity we continually fear in the background.

6
Naysaying

i. A character study

They are at one level reassuring figures. They can be relied upon to keep the budget under control; they are conscientious with officialdom, excellent at time management and well organised around regulations. They won't let a financial or procedural problem fester without letting a more senior person know; if anything, they may be too often inclined to seek clarification from the top even on small matters. They're interested in filing and forms, and have an appetite for reading the latest rules about industry standards.

However, the excessive nature of their caution comes through at many points: in meetings when new initiatives are being proposed, they habitually cite past disasters and remind people of errors of judgement that others (long since departed) once made. They work hard, from the best of motives, to undermine any feelings of excitement or spontaneity in any room they are in. One of their favourite phrases is 'that won't work'. At times, they almost give the impression that they would be pleased if certain things turned out badly. Given their attitude, colleagues generally end up going behind their backs, or trying to bypass them, rather than see their more expansive ideas ground down and quietly destroyed.

The naysayer is also resistant to change. The traditional way of doing things is always better. They can't see why it would be important to alter the desk layouts, the timing of the Wednesday meeting or the way that client enquiries are dealt with. They see themselves as the guardians of the way the company used to be in nebulously defined 'olden times'.

What the naysayer is essentially saying 'no' to in many different ways and in a variety of contexts is hope, because they are allergic to the risk that hope can entail. They are trying to disappoint themselves before the world has a chance to do it for them at a time of its own choosing. Strangely, in the process of trying to rein in risk, they create quite a few dangers for themselves. They succeed in frustrating many of their colleagues. It's hard to know how safe their position really is.

ii. Origins

No one ever begins with this degree of caution, inhibition and focus on the downside. This isn't a starting point; it is an adaptation to trauma. The manner and actions of the naysayer are guided by a theory of safety. Logically, therefore, somewhere in their past, they had a particularly intense experience of unmanageable and overwhelming risk.

Perhaps they suffered a cataclysm early on: a death in the family, bankruptcy, a war, a chaotic country, alcoholism, disgrace.... Or, more commonly, the disaster was just offstage, in the experience of a parent or caregiver, who they loved and whose suffering they experienced by proxy. In response, the naysayer developed a phobia around hazard as well as a fixed idea of how to achieve safety: by precisely following rules and procedures and rigorously disowning any exuberance and impulsiveness.

Principally, in childhood, that would have meant being obedient to teachers and the apparatus and assumptions guiding education. So long as one worked hard, kept one's head down and did well at exams (especially in the drier subjects), then there could be a chance of reaching the land of safety, whereas danger was associated with adventure, idealism and overhasty personal initiative. Hope became dangerous and safety equated with resignation and rigidity.

When change is experienced in unwelcome ways, it is understandable if familiar routines are clung to especially tightly. The natural instinct is to see the naysayer as fussy and hidebound;

in reality they are warding off dangers that we can't see but that feels as real to them as vertigo. When insisting that we stick to a particular kind of biscuit, routine or energy provider, they are not simply testing us with their inflexibility, they are maintaining a precarious hold on their sense of safety.

The naysayers' downbeat assessments are based not on dispassionate analyses of business possibilities but on an inner emotional compulsion. Their philosophy is, first and foremost, a defence against suffering.

Beneath their gruff surface, naysayers are afflicted by a near-hysterical fragility around the idea of relying on anything that might collapse on them. They twist their mental apparatus to secure themselves against the eventuality of let-down. Naysayers may look like people wedded to being realistic; in fact, they are trying to insulate themselves against pain. The origin of their stance is not worldly experience and insight; it is – more touchingly – a difficult backstory of which the legacy is a phobia around hope and novelty.

iii. Ways forward

For the naysayer, the task is to align the real risks with the risks they perceive internally. To do this we may have to do something ostensibly cruel: suggest to them that there is no such thing as safety in the terms in which they conceive of it.

Gently we might explore the idea that their choices have been guided by a fantasy of thorough security, which is, on closer inspection, a mirage. All of us are exposed to appalling accidents at every point. There will always be trade-offs and attendant tragic regrets. The apparently 'safe' paths have traps of their own – less publicised, perhaps, but every bit as real when they befall us. Caution, as much as impulsiveness, has its downsides. We should show the naysayer the risks on either side of the ledger.

Risks associated with impulsiveness	Risks associated with timidity
Bankruptcy	Mediocrity
Disgrace	The knowledge that life is elsewhere
Company collapse	Missed opportunities

It might also help to look at the many bad habits inculcated by our school education. School curricula suggest that the most important things are already known; that what is is all that could be.

They can't help but warn us about the dangers of originality. Schools teach us to deliver on rather than change expectations; to redeploy ideas rather than originate them. Behaviourally, schools teach us to respect people in authority rather than imagine – in inspiring ways – that no one knows what's going on. They want us to put up our hands and wait to be asked; to keep asking other people for permission. They imply that all will be well if we do our homework on time and obey those in charge.

To help the naysayer, or embolden ourselves, we should gently disabuse ourselves of such notions. We should not naively advocate independence of mind, but understand that risk doesn't have an obvious opposite called absolute safety. The task can't therefore be to try to avoid all risk, but to develop a faith in our capacity to survive the setbacks that riskier moves can at times inflict. Behind the fear of risk is something we might not initially expect, especially from the over-cautious naysayer: a lack of close examination of consequences. So, rather than trying to get the naysayer to think less about what could go wrong, we might usefully encourage them to find relief from their worries by being more precise about them, in order to see that even if many bad things did come to pass, they would often know how to survive, endure and recover from them.

Caution is at its best and most useful when it is in conversation with ambition. The hyper-cautious person isn't using their virtue well. They are not contributing their doubt to a debate with the upside. They have allowed themselves to believe in a myth of cost-free safety. We should sympathetically endeavour to liberate them from their idealistic yet ruinous belief in the existence of a permanently secure bunker.

7
Over-Optimism

i. A character study

They are the most relaxed person in the office. They exude a laid-back, cheerful charm. When everyone else appears tense at the start of a meeting, they are on hand with upbeat anecdotes and sincere-sounding enquiries about everyone's weekend (they were at the beach, where a friend has just bought a cottage). They take a leading role in company social events and have formed close bantering friendships with several members of staff.

But there is a problem. You once asked if they might help to sort out some issues with the conference and, in their characteristically cheerful manner, they said 'Leave it with me'. And so you did. But that wasn't the end of your worry, because a lot was at stake; unsurprisingly, you wanted to be kept in touch with progress. You sent them a few enquiries, phrased as casually as you could ('Just wondering how things might...'). Each time, the replies were long in coming, and when they did arrive, they betrayed a blithe curtness. They left you with the impression that you were a little demented for worrying so much; that a balanced person wouldn't stay up late thinking about this; that everything was in hand; and that the problem lay with you for fussing rather than with them for not addressing your anxieties. And then, three months later, the conference came around and it emerged that multiple issues had been ignored and the whole team had to scramble to sort them out and avert disaster. But by then, the breezy person was in Thailand, on a long-standing holiday on one of the southern islands.

Whenever you confront the breezy person with a doubt or fear, they sidestep it. Life, they seem always to be saying, will go on: the whole business isn't going to unravel because they didn't check certain figures or follow up on an email; things will be fine, they usually are. When they're late, they stroll in with a winning explanation; if they miss a deadline, they mention that Rome wasn't built in a day; they make it sound as if you are being pedantic for trying to keep to a timetable. They don't suffer from a nagging suspicion that they haven't quite hit the nail on the head in a report; they don't ruminate about whether they could have negotiated more favourable terms with a supplier; and they don't fret about a missed opportunity in a speech.

They are also filled with optimistic plans for the future. Their enthusiasm is mobile: at one point they were keen on expansion in South America; then they were talking about opportunities in South Korea or Norway. Now they're trying to muster support for a new piece of technology they learnt about from someone they met on a train. They don't seem to dwell on their former hopes; it's always the future that interests them. They see potential everywhere: the small local café could become a global chain or a novel they've just read could be made into a wonderful film. But their ideas seem sharply cut off from a concern with concrete steps.

These people are what we would all, at one level, wish to be a bit more like: blithe, calm, unconcerned and optimistic. Nevertheless, they are draining to work around and the cause of considerable anxiety in those who are forced to depend on them.

ii. Origins

The breezy yeasayer directs us to a rarely discussed distinction between being calm on the one hand and refusing to worry on the other. The former signals an intelligent reluctance to be dragged into fruitless concern over unnecessary or uncontrollable matters; the latter stems from a more rigid, self-focused commitment to remaining imperturbable even when the situation could be altered for the better and when others are in need of a few soothing words and a helping hand.

There is, as ever, a history to our approach to worry. We acquire an idea of how much it is right and productive to be concerned through having observed the relationship between anxiety and results in our early years. For many of us, growing up, panic correlated to a real threat, a quickening of the responses in order to avert proper disaster, of whatever size. But for the yeasayer, childhood experience provided them with a masterclass in the futility and absurdity of being anxious. Imagine if those who looked after us had been continuously panicked but, as became apparent, to no particular good end or with no tangible results to show for their fussing. If perhaps our caregivers fretted inordinately about whether we had done up enough buttons on our coats, whether they had remembered to put their bus pass in their bag, whether we'd taken an umbrella on a walk, what the weather would be like for the summer party and whether we had parted our hair correctly, there might have seemed to be across childhood a constant static of anxious electricity that crackled and disturbed us without ultimately going anywhere. The worries might not even be motivated by kindness or empathetic concern, for they might be unattuned to the real issues that are on our minds; we might have had worries but certainly not those. If it never really mattered to us how our hair was styled or what time we'd done our homework by, growing up and achieving independence might become associated with the right to stop this sort of fretting once and for all in order to adopt the calm manner that we now wear as a badge of maturity and liberation. Living life on our own terms would then be synonymous with a blithe appearance and a distaste for panic.

If you are the over-optimist, alongside your reluctance to worry may have come a powerful impulse to daydream. This is what we naturally do when reality feels at once unpleasant and beyond our control. Children are liable to go in for daydreams when they are subject to unusually difficult but also seemingly unchangeable circumstances. They daydream about making nasty teachers disappear, about finding bars of gold to change their family's fortunes or about discovering a potion to make Mummy cheer up and play with them like they used to. They might be growing up in the ambit of a beloved parent defeated by the demands of the world, and where there is not much evidence of how problems can be faced and systematically tackled through realistic steps (effort, compromise, budgeting). To survive, it may be necessary to be convinced that things will work out somehow, even when one lacks any concrete plans to help them do so. There is often nothing a child can do except hope. Dreams can be the most realistic thing they can manage; and formulating them may remain an automatic, settled habit into adulthood.

The capacity to hope for distant things and to envisage what might be is not in itself a problem; it's not at odds with practicality and careful strategic planning: in fact, ideally the two would be combined. Planning need not be dispiriting; we're trying to show how something of what's longed for can be put into action. The route to this isn't to dismiss the fantasy but to explore it more thoroughly: what would be the smallest step they could take in this direction? What is it about the ideal that's so appealing to this person and is that desired quality available in other versions? We're not aiming to crush the dreamer's soul: we're seeking to reconnect their imagination with reality.

Different kinds of experience can point us to different philosophies of worry, planning and resolution. In childhoods in which a link between periods of anxiety and good outcomes is more evident, someone might have been shouting and panicking at points, but it eventually led somewhere. There was something to show for the drama in the end. In this version, the child gets to witness a productive and sensible relationship between being concerned and changing a situation for the better. When others panicked on their behalf, they ultimately saw that they were on to something genuine and beneficial, and they were grateful. Worry was accurate, well directed, selective, proportionate and fruitful. This response is why as adults we think it fitting, at certain moments, to despair vocally, to bite our nails and to stay up into the early hours worrying intensely about the fate of our projects. We displace daydreams because we see that enough of what we long for can be secured in the real world through our own prosaic efforts.

_____ We need not so much to worry less, as to worry more accurately and scrupulously.

iii. Ways forward

Most of us are so familiar with excessive worry and are therefore so keen to tone down our misfiring jittery impulses that we are prone to miss a crucial caveat: anxiety has a critical role to play in the genesis of many good things and that, in the right doses, aimed at sincere targets, light panic deserves an honourable place within our conception of a good life. The problem is not anxiety per se, but the bewilderingly strong doses in which most of us are introduced to it and the vain or unfocused objects on which it is trained. We need not so much to worry less, as to worry more accurately and scrupulously.

To their eventual great cost, the breezy person has drawn the wrong conclusions from their own experiences. They have been initiated into unproductive worrying and come to the view that there is no such thing as good anxiety. They are, beneath their calm manner, overly and unimaginatively worried about ever being worried. The solution lies in inducting them into better kinds of worry – the sorts that have led towards just the kinds of outcomes they might themselves admire and seek to emulate. We need to enrich and add nuance to their picture of the relationship between anxiety and results.

At a societal level, part of the reason why we often miss how much anxiety lies behind certain achievements is that these feats themselves don't speak of the suffering and disquiet that they exacted from their creators. The flavoursome restaurant meal, the elegant aircraft wing, the sweeping concrete bridge, the fluent novel of ideas – none of these let on about the pain that went into them.

They stay quiet about the anguished meetings, the shouting in offices, the despair in bedrooms late at night, the moments when it seemed hopeless, not so much because they seek actively to deceive us as because the story of their fractious beginnings forms no part of their purpose. An unhurried, masterful atmosphere is indeed often crucial to their greatness: the gigantic carbon-fibre wing of the plane bends like the branch of a noble ancient oak tree in the currents of a thunderstorm; the concrete bridge makes light of its massive weight and sets its feet on either side of the desolate mountain valley with some of the finesse of a ballerina.

It is easy to be deceived. The apparently effortless, gracious achievements of others were inevitably the result of titanic efforts. Few things that attract our admiration emerge, early on in their development, from anything other than a good amount of consternation, dismay and hysteria. The breezy let themselves be fooled. They mistake all outsized efforts for the fretting and fusspotting they knew too well earlier in their lives; they grow overly committed to calm and along the way neglect the glorious work of outsized, passionate distressed attachment.

Gradually, the breezy must be shown a fuller picture of worry. We know so much about bad anxiety – the kind that wakes us up for no reason and that apprehends a disaster without cause. We need to be reminded of the good reasons for panic: the issue is not whether or not to be calm, but how to worry well. In our reflexive pursuit of calm, we have missed the real matter: how to be the good kind of worrier.

Discovering productive anxiety
in unexpected places

Bridge by Robert Maillart, Central Switzerland

787 wing by Boeing

We need to tell the blithe person that they will not lose anything meaningful by starting to worry rightly, and that their light-hearted manner, while it liberates them from some of the drawbacks of their past, is in reality a dead end and no faithful route to accomplished adulthood. We need to learn gently to unsettle our breeziest colleagues.

8
Charmlessness

i. A character study

They are accomplished at the technical side of their job. They work hard, are diligent, know everything about company systems and meeting rotas, and have an impeccable record with cash flow. But it has to be noted that they are also socially awkward. They seem incapable of even a few moments of fluent, funny or endearing small talk. They come across as brusque, formal and stiff, especially with anyone above or below them in the hierarchy. It's always something of a hurdle to be left alone in a room with them.

It shouldn't really matter, and for a long while it doesn't. But as they come to be considered for more senior, client-facing roles, the issue starts to loom larger. It is a peculiar feature of business life that major deals can at points depend on nothing more, but also nothing less, than the ability to convey an impression of warmth and likeability – a true skill as yet unaddressed by the curriculum of any business school.

It feels impossible to imagine these colleagues ever entertaining someone successfully over lunch or charming a room of strangers. Although they obey all the rules of etiquette and might dutifully offer their guests a drink or remark on a recent piece in a financial journal, they never manage to seem engaging or endearing. A lot of opportunities slip by. Their inhibitions are, in their own way, as harmful to their careers as failure in an accountancy or a legal exam, but much less well recognised as a risk.

By contrast, there is the colleague we recognise as warm,

who follows the cold person in the basic principles of politeness but manages to add an engaging and emotionally comforting ingredient to their manner. When they are arranging lunch with a client, they might suggest that, given the unusually beautiful weather, they order some sandwiches and eat them on a park bench together. When they're with an associate who has a bad back, they might plump up a cushion and slot it behind their back. They might confess to feeling intimidated by a mutual acquaintance in an adjoining industry or make encouraging 'mmm' and 'ahh' sounds to show sympathy and interest for a story they've teased out of a colleague about their insomnia. When an associate drops their folder or bumps into the elevator door by mistake, they exclaim: 'I'm so glad you did that! Usually it's me.'

On paper, the charming employee isn't any better than their stiff counterpart. But when it comes to knowing who to deploy or promote, the answer can often feel painfully obvious.

ii. Origins

Stiffness may seem like an ingrained, almost natural, disposition, but it is a treatable condition provoked by a set of somewhat misguided ideas about what other people are like and what they require from others. Our shy and charmless episodes are rooted in a sense that little of what we know about ourselves will apply to anyone else. We act in a stiff way because we do not trust that intimidating figures or new colleagues could ever share in the less edifying, more complicated or vulnerable aspects of our nature.

Those blocked around charm operate with an implicit view that the people they are attempting to please are creatures endowed with only the highest and most formal of needs. They make all kinds of assumptions about those they are trying to entertain: that they are interested exclusively in so-called serious topics; that they demand and appreciate a high degree of ceremony and convention at all times; that they will be strong, self-contained and mature enough not to have any hunger for reassurance or cosiness or fun; and that they will be without urgent physical vulnerabilities and drives, which might prove offensive if they were ever mentioned.

By contrast, the warmly polite person is always aware that a stranger (irrespective of their status or outward dignity) will have a lot in common with who they are: they will be needy, fragile, confused, bored, trapped, appetitive and susceptible. They know this about the stranger, because they never forget this about themselves.

iii. Ways forward

The solution to stiffness lies in making a crucial leap of faith: that, whatever our background or upbringing, others' minds work in much the same way as ours do.

Charming and natural-seeming people have a lot in common with the character Kanga, the tenderly maternal kangaroo in A.A. Milne's Winnie-the-Pooh books. In one of the stories, the little animals are disconcerted by the arrival in the Hundred Acre Wood of Tigger, who is big, loud, bouncy and assertive. They treat him with caution and are, we might say, coldly polite. But when Tigger finally meets Kanga, she is immediately warm with him. She thinks of him in much the same terms as she does her own child, Roo. 'Just because an animal is large, it doesn't mean he doesn't want kindness; however big Tigger seems to be, remember that he wants as much kindness as Roo,' says Kanga, in what might be a definition of the philosophy of warmth.

Sometimes it is generous to think that another person high up in another company may belong almost to another species. Collectively in business, we've taken this thought much to heart. We have internalised distance and learnt caution and formal manners.

But this can give rise to a reserve that benefits no one. The warmly polite person may not hold to an explicit theory of what they are doing, yet at root their conduct is based on an understanding that however solid and dignified someone appears on the outside, behind the scenes there will inevitably be a struggling self, potentially awkward, easily bemused, beset by physical appetites, on the verge of loneliness, longing to laugh, and frequently in need of nothing more subtle or elevated than a friendly and reassuring chat about nothing too serious.

It can seem like an act of extreme respect to imagine that others are not as peculiar and need-filled as we are. Much of our childhood experience subtly reinforces the belief that there is a category of grown-up, starting with teachers, who share in none of the child's humanity. At a certain age, we may need such an illusion to make the world feel stable. But we pay a high price in loneliness and eventual social awkwardness for this faith in the face value of authority figures. True adulthood and a warm, inviting, winning manner begin with a firmer hold on the notion that every severe, dignified and besuited person we meet must, behind the scenes, almost certainly be as human and vulnerable as we are. We should dare to address them as such when we wish to win their trust, to charm them and to do business with them.

9

Procrastination

i. A character study

What is striking about procrastination is just how many varied and creative forms it can take, and how it can affect us all at one time or another. The simplest and most familiar kind involves sitting at a desk with a blank sheet of paper, staring out of the window rather than writing our financial report, job application form or autobiography. But that is only the start of the options. Another more dynamic kind of procrastination involves developing an addiction to one thing that prevents us from doing another. We may get hooked on the Internet and check the news at four-minute intervals, to keep the news from ourselves at bay. We may do a lot of tiring sport, exhausting our bodies in the hope of not having to hear from certain parts of our minds. Then there is the procrastination that involves hyperactivity, where we work furiously on certain projects in order to avoid other, harder, ones. We can be busy and seemingly productive while, in essence, remaining as reluctant to get down to crucial tasks as someone who might have spent the afternoon gazing at the building opposite.

ii. Origins

The problem with most responses to procrastination – both from others and the procrastinator's own estimation of themselves – is that they boil the problem down to laziness. In the process, they shame the procrastinator further, rendering ever more remote the chances of them returning to the work that counts. It isn't that we procrastinate because we are self-indulgent, slothful or bad people. The truth is more complicated, more psychologically nuanced and more worthy of sympathy.

The real reason we are indolent is because we are *scared*. What we are quick to call being lazy is at heart a symptom and consequence of anxiety.

_____ The real reason we are indolent is because we are *scared*. What we are quick to call being lazy is at heart a symptom and consequence of anxiety.

iii. Ways forward

In order to help ourselves, and those around us, to work effectively, we have to find ways to reduce our fears and our anxieties around the tasks that matter to us.

Tellingly, it tends to be easy to get down to work on things that don't matter much to us. Their lack of importance encourages our lighter, more carefree and more productive sides. We find we're done with them in no time and it doesn't even feel like work; it's closer to play.

Yet the stuff that really counts, that we need done because our lives may depend on it, terrifies us into inactivity. We are so scared of failure we don't dare to make a start. At least, if we leave the task untouched, we won't need to face any risk of humiliating incapacity or incompetence. The results cannot fail to live up to our expectations if we have not begun.

This estimation of a task's importance points to how we might increase our productivity. We would be advised not to try to galvanise ourselves by reminding ourselves (or getting others to remind us) of how important a task may be: we are aware of this already and that is precisely the problem. What we need to do is to emphasise its relative unimportance in the scheme of things. So what if, in the end, we don't get the job, or lose the contract or are thought an idiot by people we care about? It happens, and it's survivable. Instead of ramping up the pressure, we must strive to turn the task from a terrifying ordeal into the only thing we'll know how to deal with calmly and energetically: a piece of play. Lessening the imagined consequences of messing up liberates us to devote to a task all the energy and talent we actually possess.

Another way to unblock ourselves (or an ambitious but stalled colleague) is to remember that, whatever we suppose, things don't need to be perfect. We can get so ambitious about how something should turn out that we grow disparaging about our own stumbling beginnings and therefore make minimal advances. We take a first step but are horrified by the rawness and amateurish quality of our output; it falls crushingly short of what we envisaged. So we down tools and slump into despair. We, who like perfection so much, cannot tolerate the gap between what we have done and the standards of the mature finished products we admire. In order to progress, we should forgive ourselves the horror of the first draft.

It can also help to bring the pressure of another – and even greater – fear to the stalled situation we dread. A major obstacle to fruitful activity is the feeling that we are immortal. We may not experience ourselves as exactly ignorant of death, but in the lackadaisical way we approach the choices and hurdles before us, in the amount that we defer and evade, we are implicitly behaving as if the business of waking every new day had privately been guaranteed to us to go on forever. Why else would we fail again and again to do what we know needs to be done? One answer might be to put a skull on our desks, as medieval philosophers and theologians did, as a reminder that life is short. The idea of death should both scare us and liberate us somewhat not to mind too much if we do hit obstacles in more ambitious ventures. If everything is doomed to end in the grave, then it might not matter much if we embark on a new task and mess up a bit. The thought of death may be simultaneously terrifying and the harbinger of a kind of light-heartedness and productive irresponsibility.

Another way to lessen our fear and so increase our output is to pretend to ourselves that we are not going to do any work, while engaging in an activity that still leaves our minds free to think. Taking a train ride, sitting in a café or going for a walk can be ideal for this. A core reason why we often can't progress with certain ideas and plans is that they are at odds with our current commitments and habits, and therefore generate anxieties about needing to change course. A new plan might, for example, reveal that we need to make some serious and possibly disruptive decisions. If we took a nascent idea seriously, we might have to leave a job or have an awkward conversation with a colleague. But on a long journey alone on a train or on a stroll on a beach, our minds, set free of our working surroundings, may be more willing to entertain these intimately challenging ideas. We can find reassurance that we are at a distance from the normal context of our lives; if we make a decision we won't have to act on it immediately. The passing countryside or the rolling waves give us a spectacle to absorb our restlessness and dread.

Lastly, to release ourselves from the shame and self-hatred that tends to accompany procrastination, we should accept an often-unmentioned truth: that procrastination affects everyone, though often only when they are alone and out of sight. This leads to a punishing and unhelpful asymmetry of knowledge. We know from the inside our own horrible habits of time wasting and evasion. But we see only the smooth, productive exteriors of others. We catch our colleagues and friends mostly in their more dynamic moments. We don't get to see how far they may be falling short of their own ambitions. It may look as if they have accomplished quite a lot, but their private experience can be of tortured frustration, in which they are acutely aware of the gap between their ambitions and their achievements.

We need to construct a more accurate and imaginative picture of how others perform. While they might present an unblemished façade of productivity, we need to imagine the long hours when their minds felt like glue, unable to get going on anything serious or demanding; their failures to confront the hard questions around an issue; the things they must have abandoned because they couldn't muster the intellectual energy to address them properly, the hours they will have spent online looking up woollen socks or holidays in Spain.

Procrastination is a problem – both for ourselves and for those we work with – but it is not a unique or even unusual problem. And it is one capable of being cured with calculated doses of fear, reassurance, confession and humour.

10
Cynicism

i. A character study

Cynicism is in many ways a healthy and necessary emotion to experience in relation to aspects of the working world. There is so much to regret and lament; so many ways in which companies and colleagues disappoint us; so much annoyance to absorb.

But we should note how, at times, cynicism moves from being an occasional sentiment to a settled character trait; how one may shift from having cynical thoughts to being a cynical person much of the time. The cynicism can flow in any number of directions: from bosses to workers; employees to managers; companies to customers. What unites the cynical stance is a refusal to see unfortunate behaviour as occasional and motivated by forces one could try to understand (and perhaps even alter), and a commitment to dismissing a given target group as forever tainted and horrid.

There is the manager-cynic, who has an extraordinarily dark take on their employees: they see a world where all staff below them are out to milk the company, moan unfairly, avoid doing any proper work, raise petty objections and have no loyalty or backbone. Then there is the employee-cynic, who makes constant wry and caustic references to authority, management, bosses, profits, hierarchy, 'the senior team' and ambition. Then there is the salesperson-cynic, who has a large and constantly renewed supply of stories against those their company serves: the idiots who don't know how to use the new website; the idiots who call up complaining that the shop is shut (even when the hours are clearly stated on the door); the idiots who accused them of having added something extra to the bill and then discovered the figure had been correct all along.

The complaints of the cynic may differ, but the underlying objection is the same: a whole group of people are dismissed as ungrateful, hysterical, pampered, paranoid and undeserving – an idea that is easy to sympathise with, clearly sometimes has truth to it, and yet remains unconstructive and often unfair.

ii. Origins

It is hopeless to try to disprove cynicism; there will always be an abundance of vivid examples to back up a catastrophic interpretation of humanity. But in order to weaken the cynical impulse, one can try to discover its origins. Cynicism seems, first and foremost, to be a defence against suffering – the kind that stems from having been too hopeful at the outset and then encountered grievous disappointment along the way.

Beneath their stern manner, cynics are trying to escape from wounded hopes: hopes that their customers would be kinder and nobler; that junior staff would be more grateful and more accommodating; that bosses would be more empathetic and more generous. Because these hopes so often went nowhere, cynics rewire their mental apparatus to secure themselves against further discouragement. They opt to disappoint themselves before the world can do it for them again at a time and in a manner of its own choosing.

iii. Ways forward

Rather than tell the cynic to cheer up, look on the bright side, or think positively, one of the ways forward might be to suggest that the cynic indulge in a healthy dose of pessimism. Rather than begin with ardent hope and then find oneself bouncing to an extreme of disappointment, a more measured approach accepts from the outset that frequent disappointment will be the norm: of course, employees will sometimes frustrate, customers will annoy, bosses will enrage. It's a miracle if it doesn't happen every day. When the gentle pessimist encounters obstacles, they don't see these as violations of the ground rules of existence, merely as a fulfilment of long-held possibilities. It is in the natural order of things that businesses are less than perfect, interactions at all levels of the company can be fraught, and that clients can be in a bad mood.

Pessimism is often seen as the enemy of good things; we miss how usefully it can provide a kindly inoculation against cynicism. It keeps our wilder hopes at bay and, in its way, offers protection against the more intense forms of anger, despair and loathing. The pessimist's advice to the cynic is that they can survive the frustration of their hopes, but that it is not so inevitable that they should avoid hope altogether. So what, in the end, if certain bosses are maddening, certain workers spoilt and certain customers imbecilic? There are others who aren't; there will be some good days after the bad ones; and if the situation is untenable, the world remains a broad place and other options are always available.

The other great solution to cynicism (as well as anger and rage) lies with an emotion seldom mentioned in the commercial world yet vital for the maintenance of any minimally endurable society: love. It sounds odd to think of love in a business context, let alone to conceive of it as something one might be expected to practise around awful people. We tend to reserve the word for lovers, close friends and our benevolent families. But we are thereby restricting our concept of love to a few privileged arenas and so misunderstand what love really entails and how relevant it can be to all areas of our lives.

We need to direct love precisely at people who aren't paragons of virtue: if we only ever love those who are conspicuously good, we won't have understood the true ambition and potential of this emotion. We reach a peak of ethical achievement precisely when we love people at their more unlovable moments.

Love can be defined as a willingness to imagine generous reasons why someone could have evolved to be graceless or cruel, a bore or maddeningly indecisive, revoltingly abrupt or haughtily condescending. It is easy but unhelpful to be unimaginative on this score, and only ever invested in concluding that others are rotten and disgusting. Picturing instead why someone might have done a regrettable deed – perhaps they got frightened; maybe they were under pressure of extreme anxiety and despair, and this was all they could manage? – helps them remain a fitting target for understanding and sympathy. The loving interpreter holds on to the idea that goodness must remain beneath the surface, along with the possibility of remorse and growth. They are committed to finding any aspect of the truth that could cast a less catastrophic light on folly and 'nastiness'.

Cynicism is a retreat – from hope, disappointment, betrayal – yet love leads us to understand that we can embrace a bigger picture: reality is always more complicated and nuanced than we might at first expect. Those who look with love understand that early pain and let-down form the backdrop to later transgressions. Bad behaviour is so often the consequence of hurt: the one who shouts did not feel heard; the one who mocks was once humiliated. From this perspective, acting badly is a response to a wound, never an initial ambition. Just as we don't readily assign a negative motive or mean intention to a child, with love we reach around for the most benevolent interpretation.

Love-thinkers view everyone as having strengths alongside their obvious weaknesses. When they encounter weaknesses, they do not conclude that this is all there is, but search a little harder for the strength to which a maddening characteristic must be twinned. We can see easily enough that someone is pedantic and uncompromising; we tend to forget, at moments of crisis, their thoroughness and honesty. In this perspective, there is no such thing as a person with only strengths; nor is there someone with only weaknesses. Where a cynic might lose cause for hope, the love-thinker finds consolation in refusing to view defects in isolation. Love is built out of a constantly renewed and gently resigned awareness that weakness-free people do not exist. We are in equal measures idiotic, mentally wobbly and flawed.

We can learn to flex the muscles of love by imagining the backstories of strangers in a way that transforms our assessment of their outward conduct. Although such a request runs (deliberately) counter to our impulses, try to come up with a backstory that could help you think more sympathetically and kindly about the following people:

- *Someone in a restaurant shouting that they've been overcharged when in fact the bill is correct.*

- *A boss who goes through a draft document with a new trainee, minutely criticising the punctuation (even though it's already 7 p.m. and the final version will be carefully checked anyway).*

- *Someone who never misses an opportunity to explain how wonderfully their children are doing.*

- *Someone who likes to draw attention to their expensive watch.*

11
Frankness

i. A character study

We recognise the frank person by their overt and unembarrassed commitment to calling a spade a spade. If an idea strikes them as ridiculous, they don't let the other person down gently. They won't say: 'That's interesting, but it may not be the right approach at the moment'; they call it 'frankly idiotic'.

In ordinary conversation, they don't have time to emit constant small signals of reassurance. They assume that everyone has a decent conception of themselves already. It doesn't strike them as worth mentioning when someone on the team has done exceptionally well: they must know it already. They don't gently say that something is fascinating if they don't really think that it is. They like to be the first to bring up what they call 'the elephant in the room'. If a colleague has delayed announcing a pregnancy, they'll ask in a collective meeting what's happening around maternity leave.

The frank person sees themselves as the lone voice of truth in a world of prevarication, dishonesty and fake sentiments. They don't think they are rude or brusque; they just admire unpolished honesty and a thorough lack of fakeness.

ii. Origins

The frank person works with a picture of what other people are like: robust, sure of themselves, with no need for reassurance or encouragement. In their mind, everyone's ego is already as big as it can feasibly be; they see danger in the other direction – in inflating people's self-regard intolerably. They don't recognise the level of vulnerability and self-doubt that most people actually have. If someone complains, they call them thin-skinned; they don't allow that everyone is internally bothered by 'frank' words but that (at great emotional cost) most of us manage to put a brave face on the situation.

Strangely, the frank individual ultimately lacks confidence, which can sound odd because they seem so sure of their opinions. But it makes sense because the frank person logically feels, in the background, that it doesn't really matter what they say or neglect to say, for no one (in their essential view of things) will be much affected or upset by their abrasive words, or really needs their support, protection or care.

The frank person could become more sensitive and kinder not by thinking less of themselves but by increasing their impression of the impact their words, glances, recommendations and advice can have; by realising that they have the power – simply through the way they put something in an email or phrase an idea in the corridor – to cast a shadow over someone's entire day.

To make an analogy, it is only people who have a secure sense of their own physical strength who will go out of their way to be gentle, because only they are aware of the injuries they could easily inflict on others with their powerful limbs. By contrast, the adolescent who badly hurts a younger sibling by mistake in a playfight hasn't learnt to understand and trust in the power of their newly grown body. Similarly, in the way they crash into their colleagues and bruise them haphazardly, the frank person betrays an inability to conceive of their own potential power. They say what they like because they don't anticipate that anyone could take it to heart too much.

iii. Ways forward

A real kindness we can do the frank person is to let them into the more easily bruised zones of our own personalities: not defensively, when we feel attacked, but as a calm, general admission. We need to let them know how fragile our hold on our self-esteem can be and how easily a weekend can be ruined by an off-hand remark.

In the process, we're revealing the normality of the lonely, frightened but often disavowed part of all our natures: we're inducting them into the universality of extreme sensitivity. Thereby, we're also pointing them to the true root of politeness: the realisation that, like us, other people are often much closer to self-hatred and self-disgust than their outward demeanour might suggest. The polite person treads gently, is cautious about what they mention to others and softens their assertions not because they are unusually moral in an abstract way, but because they know how easily all of us can bruise and be bruised.

Exercise

We are all very sensitive without realising this about one another. What are some of the smallest things you have been quite badly upset by? What have others said to you that you remember to this day but that might (to a frank person) have appeared negligible?

Share the list with a friend and hear theirs in turn.

12
Immaturity

i. A character study

There often isn't much time for the finer nuances of psychology in our day-to-day lives. We tend to be too busy keeping companies afloat, fulfilling customers' expectations and striving to make the next month's figures in order to have the energy left to pin subtle labels to the warps in behaviour we notice in our colleagues. When we collide with a problematic person, we tend to capture what irks us in a general way. We might call them 'neurotic' or 'mad', 'difficult' or 'a headcase'.

It's understandable that we should reach for a catch-all term. However, there are better and worse words with which to generalise. The most effective, comprehensive and humane is also one of the simplest: immaturity. If we wanted to sum up most of what is askew with ourselves and our fellow troublesome humans, we could do worse than to define our collective deficiencies and insanity under the umbrella term 'immature'.

It is out of immaturity that we rage and slander, that we are meek and uncreative, that we grow suspicious and panicky, that we connive and betray, that we are insulted and offended.

ii. Origins

Why have we not developed as we should have? Why are we not as properly grown-up as we might be? If we wanted to further generalise about the origins of human fragility and woe, we could point above anything else to two problematic dynamics that operate in almost all our most regrettable behaviours: *low self-worth* and *low trust in others*. These two phenomena seem best able to explain why living with ourselves and others can prove so difficult.

Where there is low self-worth, a litany of troubles follow:

Low self-worth leads to:

- Inability to take criticism.
- Inability to disagree firmly but calmly.
- Paranoid fear that others hate us.
- If we are no good, disaster or punishment must come our way.
- We cannot show our true selves: stiffness.
- What we really think won't appeal to anyone: lack of creativity or originality.
- Defensive grandiosity and arrogance.

And where there is low trust in others, a range of adjoining difficulties arise:

Low trust in others leads to:

- Inability to trust those who give us feedback.
- Inability to teach others about what we feel, want and think.
- A fear that others are primed to attack and denigrate us.
- Others have let us down and might do so again: conservatism and rigidity.
- Others have not been charmed by us and won't be in the future: shyness, reserve or diffidence.

Unsurprisingly, both of these dynamics can be traced back to flawed developments in childhood. It's an unfortunate vulnerability in our make-up that we cannot value ourselves until we have been valued by someone else; we learn to like who we are because someone, way back, first liked who we were. It was through their enthusiasm and resilient care for us that we gradually grew able to internalise a positive self-image and then acquired the tools to care for ourselves and others, even when the world beyond was ambiguous or hostile. This caregiver's kindly supportive voice became the way we learned to speak to ourselves at moments of crisis. As a result of love, we have the strength to hear criticism; we can apply boundaries and push back against unfair treatment; we don't await punishment or disaster; we can be ourselves in company and our minds are creative and unafraid of their depths.

Similarly, trust in others is the gift of a good childhood; the result of a positive relationship with one or two people in our formative years. When we entered the kitchen – not every time, but enough times to form a protective layer over our ego – they looked up and lit up. We trusted them. If there was something that worried us, we knew they would listen and try to help. They would never humiliate or attack us. They were on our side. We could show them our darker, more complex aspects without fearing that we'd disgust them. They could deal with the odd tantrum and so taught us about forgiveness. Their resilient affection, no matter what, is the emotional bedrock upon which all our later poise and confidence is based. Thanks to this one good relationship, we can have multiple other good relationships. We can trust that people in general aren't out to hurt us. We have enough faith in the power of communication that we can explain what we want and how we feel in a calm, steady way that's likely to be heard. We aren't crippled in social situations. We don't fear change or new initiatives because we have first-hand experience of things broadly working out.

_____ It's an unfortunate vulnerability in our make-up that we cannot value ourselves until we have been valued by someone else.

iii. Ways forward

In dark moments, it can be tempting to assume that if we have not had adequate love in the early years and have lacked experience of good relationships, we are done for. The truth is less sombre. We will face great difficulties – a kind of tax on our whole lives exacted by our childhoods that other, luckier people might never have to pay – but we can follow three routes to ameliorate our sorrows.

Firstly, we need to understand the past. This is less obvious than it might sound. It takes a great deal of courage to explore, at the necessary level of detail, what really happened to us and why. The mind's temptation is to flee such uncomfortable material for easier subjects, but recovery requires a proper engagement with the humiliations and agonies of yesteryear.

Secondly, we need to be able to commune around our wounds with others who have gone through the same or similar things. We need to ensure that we are not alone with our pains and that we build connections with fellow sufferers.

Thirdly – a related point – we need to build reparative relationships. If we were not properly loved then, we need to find people who can love us properly now. This may not be easy; depending on our history, we might reject appropriate candidates who offer themselves. But our relationships with others will help us both to lessen our suspicion of ourselves and to see that the world won't always reject our ideas, try to mock us or have no time for us.

Nowadays, people tend to pride themselves on their capacity for hard work. There is no harder work than that outlined above. It will not necessarily lead to a fatter pay packet or promotion, but it might be the most valuable work we undertake in terms of its effect on ourselves and those around us.

Part 3
Towards Harmony

1. Normalising Difficulty

One of the worst ways to try to get anyone to evolve is to imply that their difficulties might be theirs and theirs alone. Pinning instances of emotional immaturity down to particular people only makes them feel singled out and ashamed and therefore liable to respond with irritation or denial. If the goal is to improve emotional maturity, the sole effective strategy is to describe the ambition in universal, generic and honourable terms – not on the basis that anyone has done anything 'wrong' but because we all require help, from the CEO to the recruit who joined last week. We won't develop the courage to address our quirks until we witness everyone around us equally engaged by, and prepared to brave, the task.

Framing emotional evolution as a general priority isn't just expedient politics, it is also true to the facts. Every human being, however accomplished and skilled they might be, can be counted on to remain emotionally immature in myriad ways, and so can benefit from self-exploration and reflection. There is no such thing as a proper adult, only humans marked by a fascinatingly uneven blend of qualities ranging from confidence and trust to suspicion and self-hatred. It is not, and never has been, an option for anyone to be wholly grown-up and balanced.

In the circumstances, companies seeking to raise their emotional intelligence should in good faith sign up to a charter, relevant to all their employees:

A charter of emotional intelligence

- Everyone who has ever lived is, and has been in certain areas, immature.

- Everyone would benefit from attempting to develop their emotional intelligence.

- Everyone should welcome the opportunity to start on a path towards greater self-acceptance and greater trust in others.

- Our immaturities make us all tricky to work with.

- We are committed to trying to understand our immaturities, to admitting them to others with grace and humour, to listening to well-meaning feedback about them, and to overcoming them where and when we can, supported by our colleagues.

- We accept that the goal of emotional maturity is structurally no different from an ambition for physical health, and that both require regular training and a degree of effort.

- We won't always succeed, but we are devoted to trying.

To build on this, when it comes to interviewing candidates for positions, an emotionally intelligent corporation wouldn't just ask about universities and grades. It would also hand prospective candidates a card containing a list of challenging emotional traits and then ask them to fill in, on a scale of 1–10 (0 not being an option), the doses they might feel themselves to possess. (An adjoining column would show how the CEO had filled in the same card, to provide reassurance that they were not being singled out, and that immaturity is universal.)

The exercise would demonstrate that all of us suffer from emotional immaturities to some degree. The afflictions may be significant in some areas, but being less than psychologically perfect is not incompatible with being effective as well as decent, kind and interesting.

Challenging psychological trait	My strength of trait on a scale of 1-10	CEO's answer
Defensiveness		8
Poor teaching		6
People pleasing		4
Paranoia		8
Panickiness		9
Naysaying		1
Over-optimism		3
Charmlessness		2
Procrastination		2
Cynicism		2
Frankness		4
Immaturity		1

2. Plotting for Emotional Growth

As part of a mission to help colleagues evolve, one might hand around a couple of exercises, requesting that respondents circle a variety of terms and adjectives.

Exercise 1: With time, I hope I can grow more...

(Ring 3 words that feel most applicable)

Open-minded   *Encouraging*

Patient

Self-accepting

Resolute

Serene

Adventurous

Realistic

At ease

Decisive

Hopeful

Forgiving   *Kind*

Exercise 2: With time, I hope I can grow less...

(Ring 3 terms that feel most applicable)

Averse to criticism

Impatient with team-members

Angry at customers and colleagues

Accommodating but inauthentic

Convinced others are out for me

Dreamy

Jittery

Negative and rigid

Socially awkward

Reluctant to do the hardest, most necessary things

The organisation might even put on a range of workshops designed to honour the desire for evolution and maturation. Those seeking to grow out of a rigid mindset might head for a session on Confidence; someone with a panicky mindset might be directed to a lunchtime session on Calm. The key point would be that everyone would study something, and doing so would be viewed as a natural step in seeking to become a better colleague and a wiser human.

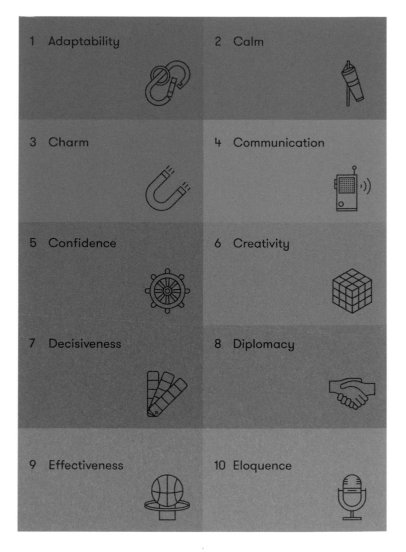

1 Adaptability

2 Calm

3 Charm

4 Communication

5 Confidence

6 Creativity

7 Decisiveness

8 Diplomacy

9 Effectiveness

10 Eloquence

11 Empathy

12 Entrepreneurship

13 Innovation

14 Leadership

15 Objectivity

16 Playfulness

17 Purpose

18 Resilience

19 Self-awareness

20 Supportiveness

Those who wished to deepen their exposure to emotional learning still further might take up their organisation on an offer of subsidised on-to-one psychotherapy. Far from being a sign that one was in trouble, seeking therapy would be taken as a sign of particular integrity and devotion to one's career; like a bonus, it might perhaps be a gift from a company seeking to reward excellence.

An emotionally intelligent office would also think hard about its away-days. Organisations tend to recognise that encountering colleagues outside the office can help the atmosphere between them in the office. That is why otherwise sober managers will organise games of table tennis, trips to the forest for paintballing, or tournaments of egg-and-spoon races. There is an unfocused hope that seeing someone we normally encounter only in a meeting or at a computer terminal playing an unexpectedly good backhand or falling into the mud will somehow ease tensions on the supply chain analysis or the development of next year's marketing strategy.

The hunch isn't wrong. The more we emerge as full human beings in the minds of others, the more likely they are to be patient with our foibles and forgiving of our blunders. We are likely to remain calmer, kinder and more sympathetic towards people whose backstories we know; when we can see a little of how someone must have come to be the way they are and appreciate the pressures, ambitions and misfortunes that shaped them. We would ideally know a substantial amount about where our colleagues grew up, how their parents behaved around them, and perhaps even what they looked like as a child (it tends to be hard to talk intemperately with someone once you've seen a picture of them standing in the garden, aged two and a half, in dungarees, holding a red fire truck and grinning at the camera with chocolate-smeared cheeks).

That said, at present, most away-days only accidentally help us to mutually reveal parts of our psyche and our past upon which patience and forgiveness can rest. A specially designed psychological away-day could reach the target in a more systematic way.

Schedule: A psychological away-day

9–10 a.m.	Card exercise to foster sympathy and forgiveness
10–10.30 a.m	Break
10.30–11.30 a.m	Childhood photo/video session
11.30–1 p.m.	Introduction to psychotherapy
1–2 p.m.	Lunch
2–4 p.m.	'How I remain immature': group discussion
4–4.30 p.m.	Break
5–6 p.m.	'How I would like to change': group discussion
	End

Extract: Card exercise to foster sympathy and forgiveness

Gather with your team to take it in turns to answer the following questions from a pack of cards:

Round 1:

1. Describe what it would have been like to meet you when you were six years old.

2. Did you have any pets when you were growing up? What kind were they? How about now?

3. Do you have any siblings? If so, how do you feel about them?

4. In what ways, if any, did you rebel as a teenager?

5. What did you especially like to eat when you were growing up?

6. Describe a particularly memorable childhood holiday.

Round 2:

1. Did you have a stuffed toy that was important to you when you were little? Can you describe it?

2. When you were growing up did you have any thoughts, or fantasies, about the kind of job you might have as an adult?

3. Who was the kindest person you knew when you were a child?

4. What didn't really go right in your childhood?

5. What are you grateful for in your childhood?

6. What did your parents (or family) teach you about work?

Round 3:

1. What were your parents good at?

2. What were your parents not so good at?

3. What do you miss from childhood?

4. What would you like to go back and correct in the past?

5. What did you think was a particularly good game to play when you were little?

6. If you could go back and reassure the younger you about something, what would it be?

3. Conclusion

Not getting on too well with people at work may be a source of personal unhappiness, but it is not always the result of coincidence or error. It can be a deliberate strategy for an organisation to bring together people of different temperaments who can complement each other and balance out their respective flaws. Offices need a few introverts to act as a counterweight to the extroverts; a handful of cautious people to dampen the undue haste of the impulsive; some breezy optimists to match the gloom of the naysayers. This may make the atmosphere uncomfortable at times, but it isn't in itself a sign that things have gone wrong. If we can sincerely claim to like everyone in our office, it is normally a sign that the organisation might not be around for much longer, so unitary and imbalanced is its talent base. A degree of conflict, tension, disagreement and suspicion of the 'odd' people in the adjoining team form part of the necessary static of the well-functioning office.

That said, we have in general suffered unnecessarily and for too long. Work need not be a realm of interpersonal suffering, and our relationships with our co-workers need not forever be mired in suspicion and resentment. We can move beyond gossip and resignation and into the age of the emotionally intelligent office, where, with the help of insights from psychotherapy, we can take steps towards becoming the slightly more mature, effective and serene humans we long and deserve to be.

The School of Life
for Business

These essays are thought pieces based on the topics covered by The School of Life for Business. We teach twenty emotional skills to help businesses thrive in the modern economy. We work with businesses to help employees function better together – to form more engaged teams, be more productive, dynamic, and work together in more innovative and entrepreneurial ways. We build emotional skills programmes for each organisation we work with, delivered by a world class faculty.

For more information, see:

www.theschooloflife.com/business

List of works

P30

Hermann Rorschach, *Hermann Rorschach Inkblot Test*, 1932, Science History Images / Alamy Stock Photo

Picture credits